P9-DMG-963

The Basics of
SHOTGUN SHOOTING

Third Edition

Produced by the Education and Training Division

A Publication of the National Rifle Association of America

Third Edition – January, 1985
ISBN-13: 978-0-935998-41-2
ISBN-10: 0-935998-41-1

© 1985 The National Rifle Association of America

All rights reserved. Printed in the United States of America. This book may not be reproduced in whole or in parts by mechanical means, photocopying, electronic reproduction, scanning, or any other means without written permission. For information, write: Training Department, National Rifle Association of America, 11250 Waples Mill Road, Fairfax, VA. 22030.

NR40830EF13360 (7-08 Revised)

FOREWORD
Getting The Most From This Book

This book has one goal – to lead the learner through the steps necessary to perform the basics skills of shotgunning; to guide the beginner to the door marked "shotgunning opportunities" and to provide the means of opening that door. In order to achieve this goal, you'll need to understand one of the basic learning concepts used in the book's preparation.

It is the idea of learning "simple" skills before attempting more "complex" or difficult ones.

Beginning with the simple aspects of an activity allows you *to learn more quickly*, to enhance the likelihood of *initial achievement* and *to build confidence* in your ability to perform the skill. This provides a strong foundation from which to successfully pursue the many shotgun activities.

Too many beginners make the mistake of picking up a shotgun and shooting away at all kinds of moving targets. This is akin to diving into the deep end of the pool on your first attempt at swimming. You wouldn't do that – or at least not but once! You would start at the shallow end and get comfortable with being in the water. You'd learn to put your head under, then on to floating, kicking and eventually, a simple arm stroke. As you learn to put them together, you would attempt to swim in the shallow end, gaining confidence by going a little further each time. Finally, after considerable practice (and only when you feel ready) you would move to the deep end to test your new skills. Shotgun shooting is no different. If you're to be successful in learning to shoot, a step-by-step procedure must be used. This book utilizes just such a procedure.

Considered individually, each step is relatively simple. Combined with the right shotgun, target, ammunition and practice (like the beginning swimmer moving to the deep end), you will be ready to shoot, and hit, your first series of targets.

Only after practice at this level and reinforcement of basic skills should you move on to more "complex" targets of shooting activities. This approach to shotgunning has withstood the test of time and practical application by beginners, as well as experienced shooters and instructors. Knowing this concept allows you to better utilize this book in achieving your goals.

It is sufficient to know at this point that anyone with a desire to do so can learn to hit "flying targets" in a surprisingly short period of time – and, it is toward that specific end that this book is written.

ACKNOWLEDGEMENTS

An author rarely, if ever, writes a book by himself and *The Basics of Shotgun Shooting* is no exception. It reflects the concepts and thoughts of instructors, coaches and shooters, both known and unknown, who have through the years refined the information and skills used in shotgunning.

The primary author of this book is Wayne Sheets, Former Director of NRA's Education and Training Division and former shotgun instructor and coach at the Rochester Institute of Technology.

The National Rifle Association gratefully acknowledges some of the many NRA Certified Shotgun Instructors and Training Counselors who contributed to the preparation of this book.

John Beuning, M.D. and Maureen Beuning, Youth Shooting Instructors and Leaders

Burl Branham, U.S. Olympic Shotgun Team Coach and U.S. Army Marksmanship Unit Shotgun Team Coach

Robert Case, Ph. D., Skeet Coach – NRA National Junior Olympic Camp and Physical Education Professor, Indiana University

William Christy, Ed. D., Virginia 4-H Shooting Sports Program Coordinator, Virginia Polytechnic Institute and State University

Richard Dietz, Product Information Manager, Remington Arms, Co.

Lester Gephart, Shotgunner and Hunter par excellence

Arthur Goodwin, Shotgun Instructor, Rochester Institute of Technology

Don Haldeman, Olympic Trap Gold Medalist

John Linn, Trap Coach – NRA National Junior Olympic Shooting Camps, and Physical Education Professor, George Mason University

Kay Ohye, Instructor, Coach and nine time Trap All-American

Walter Walla, Ph. D., Shotgun Program and Youth Instructor

INTRODUCTION

All pastimes have their "basics" – the necessary first steps without which nothing else works. In shooting, it's a combination of knowing your firearm, the acquisition of basic shooting skills, and a large helping of the right attitude.

Shotgun shooting is, quite possibly, the most basic form of marksmanship. During our nation's early pioneering era, many settlers relied on the shotgun to keep meat on the table and provide a measure of security in the home. They had to know how their firearms worked, how to use them skillfully, how to maintain them in good working order, and how to shoot with utmost respect for their own safety and that of others.

Shotguns have changed since then. They've become more efficient, easier to use and their applications are primarily for sporting purposes in today's society. But the basic requirements of effective shotgun shooting have not changed. People today pursue the sport of shotgun shooting for a variety of reasons. Some aspire to excel on the clay target range. Others enjoy the special thrill and challenge of stalking game in the field. Whatever your motivation happens to be, this manual is designed to provide you with the basic information you'll need to make your introduction to the exciting world of shotgun shooting as safe and gratifying as possible.

Shotgun shooting is, above all, fun. You can, however, only experience the true enjoyment of shooting accurately and safely if you're in full command of the fundamentals of shotgun shooting. In the following pages, we'll take you through all the details inherent in successful shotgunning. We'll show you how your shotgun functions, how to go about selecting one that's right for you, how to care for it and most important of all – how to use it safely. We'll acquaint you with the simple but necessary shooting fundamentals. And of equal importance, we'll introduce you to some of the many ways you can find others who share your particular interests, and thus become a full participant in the shotgun shooting sports.

Followed carefully, *The Basics of Shotgun Shooting* can be your key to a sport that can last a lifetime. Read on and find out how.

CONTENTS

x

PART ONE:
KNOWING
YOUR
SHOTGUN

▆▆▆ 1. HOW YOUR SHOTGUN WORKS

Like any other skill involving the use of mechanical equipment, your introduction to shotgun shooting must begin with a knowledge of the equipment involved. Knowing you shotgun is the first step to knowing how to shoot. Equally fundamental is your awareness of the important responsibility you must accept each time you handle your shotgun.

The shotgun is a carefully engineered, reliable piece of sporting equipment. Unlike so many of today's mechanical items, it is built to last a lifetime. By itself, the shotgun poses no greater threat to person or property than any other machine. It is only when it is placed in the hands of someone unfamiliar with its proper use, or so callous as to be disrespectful of the simple rules of firearm safety, that the shotgun can become an implement of potential harm. It's simple: if you understand how your gun works and how to care for it and if you're willing to show it all due respect in handling, shooting it will be pleasurable and rewarding.

Let's begin with a simple definition. The shotgun differs from other forms of firearms in that it fires a number of projectiles called *shot* instead of a single projectile. Once they are expelled from the gun, these projectiles start spreading out. The area covered by the shotgun's *shot pattern* is, therefore, considerably larger than the hole carved by a single bullet fired from a rifle or pistol. Consequently, shotguns are generally the firearms of choice in shooting a moving target. However, shotguns are often used like rifles with *rifled slug* (single projectile) ammunition when hunting big game at close range. If you plan to use your shotgun as a rifle, you'll need to study *The Basics of Rifle Shooting* manual. The basic skills used are the same as those for rifle.

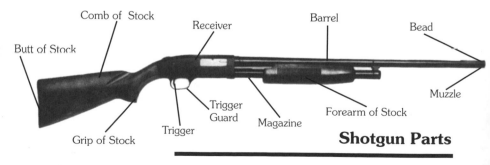

Shotgun Parts

Three major assembly groups compose the shotgun – *the stock, the barrel,* and *the action.*

THE STOCK

The *stock* serves as the shotgun's handle. It has a special significance in proper shooting. It is carefully designed to allow you to point and shoot the shotgun accurately. Each part of the stock has a special name.

The *butt* is the rear end of the stock. It's the part that rests against your shoulder when you point the shotgun.

The *comb* is the part of the stock which is brought to your cheek as you assume the shooting position.

The *grip* is the part of the stock held with the trigger hand. It is sometimes referred to as the "small of the stock" because it is where the stock narrows.

The part of the stock that lies under the barrel is called the *forearm*. On most shotguns, the forearm is separate from the rest of the stock.

THE BARREL

The *barrel* is the metal tube through which the shot passes on its way to the target. The inside portion of the barrel is called the *bore*. The diameter of the bore will vary depending on the design and use of the gun. Most shotgun bores are designated by a term known as *gauge*. The smaller the gauge number, the larger the bore size.

Starting with the largest bore, modern shotguns are available in 10, 12, 16, 20, and 28 gauge. The lone exception to this measuring system is the .410 *bore* shotgun often inaccurately referred to as the .410 gauge; it is actually a 67 gauge. This, the smallest of the modern shotguns, has a bore measured by the same standards as rifles and pistols. The .410 shotgun has a bore that is 410/1,000 of an inch in diameter.

Modern shotguns are loaded at the rear (or *breech*) end of the barrel by the insertion of a round of ammunition known as a shotshell. That portion of the barrel into which the *shotshell* is placed is known as the *chamber*. In order to be safe, the size and shape of the chamber must match that of the size shell for which your gun is designed. The front of the barrel – through which the shot exits the shotgun – is called the *muzzle*.

Popular Shotgun Shells

10 12 20 28 .410

Most shotguns have, near the muzzle, a constriction called the *choke*. It serves a very important purpose. Since shot begins to spread out immediately upon exiting the muzzle, the more constricted the shot is at the time it is expelled, the further it will travel as a compact group. This constriction is determined by the extent of the choke. The greater the choke, the greater the constriction and, generally, the greater the effective range of the gun and shot pattern.

Most commonly, a *full choke* shotgun barrel has the most constriction and the greatest range. At close range, however, a full choke shot pattern may be too small to consistently hit moving targets or so dense that game is ruined in hunting. *Modified choke* enables somewhat less constriction. *Improved cylinder choke* provides for even less constriction, and therefore a shot pattern that widens out quicker than the preceding two. Shotgun barrels that have no choke at all are referred to as *cylinder bore*. Generally, choke designations are indicated on the outside of the barrel.

4

Chokes and Their Function

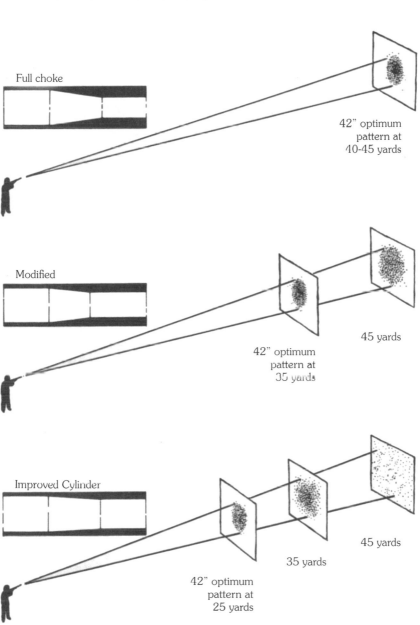

Full choke

42" optimum
pattern at
40-45 yards

Modified

45 yards

42" optimum
pattern at
35 yards

Improved Cylinder

45 yards

35 yards

42" optimum
pattern at
25 yards

Many companies today manufacture shotguns with *interchangeable screw-in chokes*. Or, a single device known as an *adjustable choke* can be placed on the end of a barrel. This choke device allows different choke selections to be made simply by adjusting it to the desired setting. Both of these options are good if one gun is to serve multiple purposes.

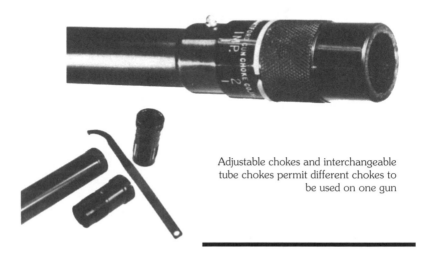

Adjustable chokes and interchangeable tube chokes permit different chokes to be used on one gun

Unlike most other modern firearms, the sighting mechanism on shotguns is rather simple. One, and sometimes two, beads are positioned onto the top of the barrel to help the shooter mount the gun properly. Some shotguns also have a flat *rib* running the length of the barrel.

THE ACTION

The moving parts which allow you to load, fire and unload the shotgun are known as the action. Most of these parts are housed in a metal frame called a *receiver*. Many different methods have been devised for operating the action. Among the most common types are *hinge, pump, semi-automatic and bolt*. In each case, however, the ultimate function is basically the same.

By operating the action, in most cases you are causing the *firing pin spring* to compress. With the action open, a shot shell can be inserted into the chamber at the breech end of the barrel. To open or close the action on many firearms requires the activation of the *"action release"* button or lever.

Loading is done by inserting a shot shell in the chamber or magazine. After loading, the action is closed and locked. Closing the action on most shotguns means the gun is *cocked* and ready for firing. This is when the *safety* should be placed in the "on" position, and, of course, it must be moved to the "off" position immediately before firing.

Once the gun is cocked, the *trigger* can be pulled at the appropriate moment. Pulling the trigger causes the *firing pin* to be driven forward. When the firing pin strikes the base of the shell, the shot shell will fire.

Re-opening the action after the shot is fired will allow removal of the empty shell case. On most shotguns, opening the action will cause the fired case to be ejected from the chamber automatically. On some, the casing must be removed by hand. Once this is accomplished, a new shot shell can be loaded, the action closed and the gun fired once again.

ACTION TYPES

Pump The actions of pump-action shotguns are opened and closed by "pumping" the forearm of the stock back and forth. Pump actions are sometimes called "slide" actions.

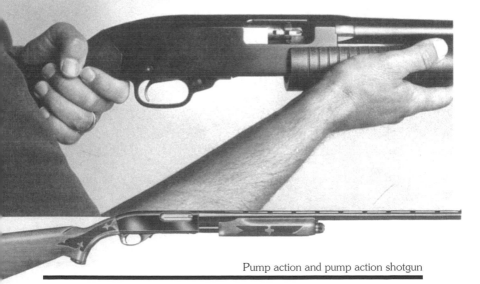

Pump action and pump action shotgun

Hinge

Similar to the movement of a door hinge, the hinge action can be opened when the release lever is pushed to one side. This separates the *standing breech block* from the barrel. Many shotguns of this type have two barrels and, based on placement, are referred to as both "over and unders" or "side by sides." They also come with just one barrel and are generally referred to as a "single barrel."

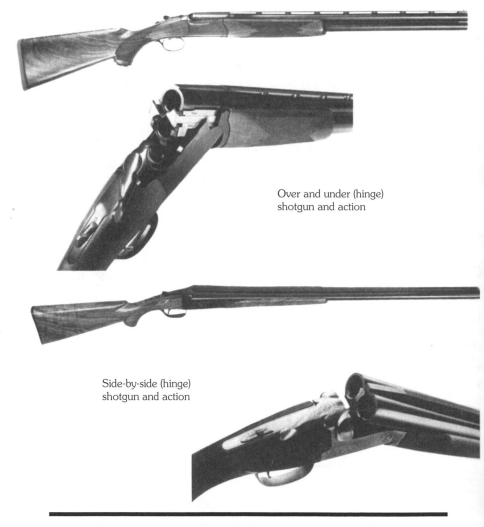

Over and under (hinge)
shotgun and action

Side-by-side (hinge)
shotgun and action

Semi-automatic   This type of action is appropriately also known as *auto-loading*. It operates automatically when the shot is fired. When a shot is fired, gas from the burning gunpowder provides the energy needed to operate the action and load the next shell. This type of action delivers less recoil to the shooter.

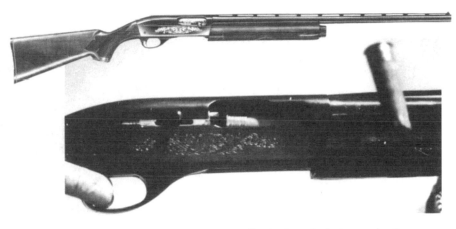

Semi-automatic shotgun and action

Bolt   A bolt action shotgun operates in the same lift, pull and push sequence employed in operating a common door bolt. It even looks like one.

Bolt action and bolt action shotgun

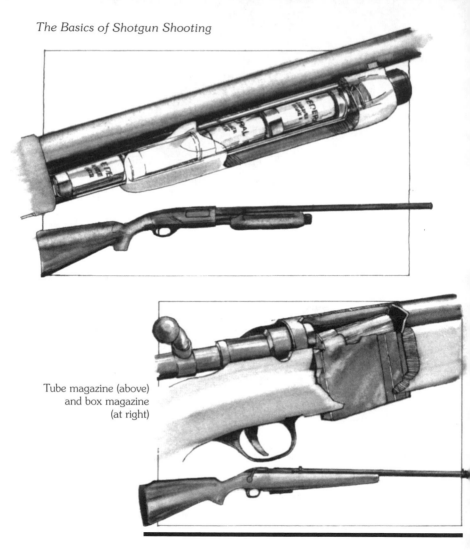

Tube magazine (above)
and box magazine
(at right)

THE MAGAZINE

Most shotgun actions can be loaded manually using one shell at a time. Many, however, have a *magazine* to expedite loading. The magazine is a container attached to the gun into which several shells can be placed. If loaded, closing the action on shotguns equipped with a magazine will allow a new shell to be pushed forward into the chamber. The gun can be fired successively until the magazine is empty.

Magazines are generally of two types. The most common is a "tube" type positioned under the barrel. The second is a "box" type located directly under the receiver.

THE SAFETY

Regardless of the type of action employed, most modern shotguns come equipped with a mechanical *safety* that, when engaged in the "on" position, should prevent the gun from firing. Safeties, as the names imply, help guard against unwanted firing and are normally used when carrying a loaded shotgun. Under no circumstances, however, should they be used as a substitute for good safety habits and shooting judgment. As mechanical devices, safeties are subject to malfunction. Therefore, even when the safety is in the "on" position, the responsible shooter always treats his gun as if firing were possible.

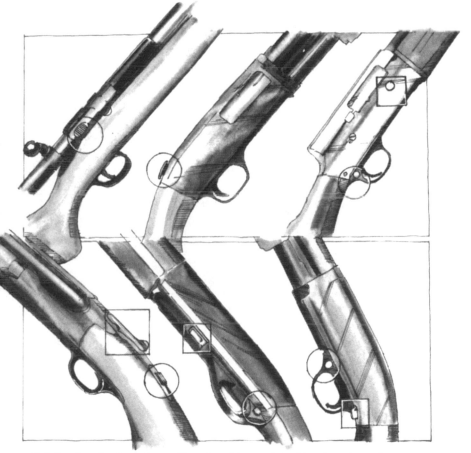

Safeties ○ and action releases □ are found in a variety of locations depending on the shotgun's make and manufacturer

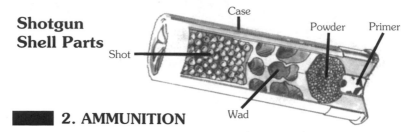

Shotgun Shell Parts

Case · Powder · Primer · Shot · Wad

■■■ 2. AMMUNITION

The modern shotgun shell contains the five components required for firing the shot. These components are the case, primer, powder, wad and shot:

- The shell *case* is the outer container for all other ammunition parts. It is typically made of plastic or paper with a metal base.
- The *primer* is contained in the middle of the shell's base where the firing pin will strike.
- The *powder charge* is located above the primer to allow easy combustion from the flame created by the initial ignition of the priming compound.
- A plastic or fiber *wad* separates the shot from the powder. It forms a seal allowing the gases created by the burning powder to push the shot uniformly down the barrel.
- The *shot* are located in the front end of the shell. Shot are small, round projectiles usually made of lead or steel. Some shot are plated with a harder metal. Depending on the weight of the shot charge and the shot size, a shell may contain anywhere from six to more than 1,300 pellets.

To fully understand these components, you must understand the way modern firearms work.

SHOT SIZE		
Identification Number	Shot Diameter	Number of Shot in and Ounce
#9 ●	.08	585
#8 ●	.09	410
#7½ ●	.095	350
#6 ●	.11	225
#5 ●	.12	170
#4 ●	.13	135
#2 ●	.15	90

APPROXIMATE NUMBER OF
SHOT IN VARIOUS LOADS

Shot Size	2 oz.	1⅞ oz.	1⅝ oz.	1½ oz.	1⅜ oz.	1¼ oz.	1⅛ oz.	1 oz.	⅞ oz.	¾ oz.	½ oz.
#9	1170	1097	951	877	804	731	658	585	512	439	292
#8	820	769	667	615	564	513	462	410	359	308	205
#7½	700	656	568	525	481	437	393	350	306	262	175
#6	450	422	396	337	309	281	253	225	197	169	112
#5	340	319	277	255	234	213	192	170	149	128	85
#4	270	253	221	202	185	169	152	135	118	101	67
#2	180	169	158	135	124	113	102	90	79	68	45

Shotguns "fire" by means of a chain reaction that begins when the trigger is pulled and ends when the shot are expelled from the barrel. The first step occurs when the firing pin strikes the primer, causing its priming compound to ignite. The flame generated by the primer ignites the powder charge. The rapidly burning powder produces a high volume of gases. Gases under pressure will seek the path of least resistance. Since the breech end of the barrel is blocked and the muzzle end is open, this path will take the gases through the bore and out the muzzle. Standing in the way of the gases, however, are the wad and shot. But since they give the least resistance, the gases push them along as they travel to the muzzle. All this is done in a split second – at a velocity more than 1,250 feet per second. This velocity diminishes as the shot travels until the shot falls to earth at a range of 300 yards or more. After 40-60 yards, however, the shot has lost velocity and energy and the pattern has become so widely dispersed that it is not reliable to effectively hit most moving targets.

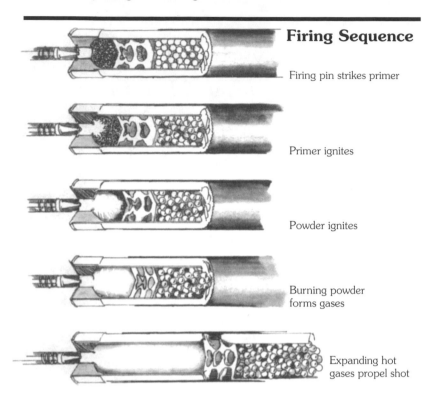

Firing Sequence

Firing pin strikes primer

Primer ignites

Powder ignites

Burning powder forms gases

Expanding hot gases propel shot

AMMUNITION MALFUNCTIONS

Shotgun shooters should be aware of the following possible shotshell malfunctions:

Misfire – a *failure* of the shotshell to fire after the primer has been struck by the firing pin.

Hangfire – a *perceptible delay* in the ignition of a shotshell after the primer has been struck by the firing pin.

Squib load – development of less than normal pressure or velocity after ignition of the shotshell.

When a shotshell fails to fire immediately, it will not be known at first whether the problem is a *misfire* or a *hangfire*. Keep the shotgun pointed in a safe direction – a hangfire condition might exist and the shotshell could still fire. Don't attempt to open the action of the gun to remove the shotshell for at least 30 seconds.

If anything unusual is noticed when a shot is fired, such as a difference in recoil or noise, stop firing immediately. A *squib load* may have been fired. Keep the muzzle pointed in a safe direction and unload the gun. *Check to be sure that the chamber is empty.* Then, with the action open, carefully run a cleaning rod through the barrel to be sure that it is not obstructed. (Squib loads can result in the wad failing to exit the barrel. If the wad is lodged in the barrel, the firing of another shot could cause serious injury or damage.)

USE THE RIGHT AMMUNITION

The kind of ammunition you use will depend both on the kind of shooting you intend to do and on the gauge of the gun. Use only those shotshells that are appropriate for the shotgun. In most cases, modern shotguns are stamped on the barrel to indicate the gauge and length of the shotshell. The base of the shell case is also commonly marked with the gauge of the cartridge and its manufacturer. Be absolutely sure these match.

Use the proper gauge of ammunition for your shotgun – take time out to check the identification of box, shells and shotgun

Ammunition manufacturers have the user's best interest in mind. They generally mark the boxes in which they pack their products with the gauge, shot size, powder charge, the amount of shot and shell length. Purchase only the gauge and length appropriate for the gun, and a shot size and powder charge suitable for the intended use.

AMMUNITION AND CHOKE SUGGESTIONS

Game	Suggested Shot Size	Suggested Chokes	What Experienced Shotgunners Say...
Ducks	5,6 2, 4, 6 (steel)	Modified – for Pass Shooting; Improved Cylinder – Over Decoys	Use No. 2 steel shot for long range and pass shooting. For normal range –or No. 4 shot while some hunters use No. 6 _ shot for closer range shooting over decoys.
Geese	BB, 2, (steel)	Modified	Goose hunters need wallop so they use the big loads with large shot. Many hunters prefer No. 2 shot for a denser pattern at short ranges over decoys. Lead shot is illegal for waterfowl.
Pheasants	5,6,7 1/2	Improved Cylinder – Close Cover; Modified or Full – For Long Cornfield Shots	For cornfield shooting where long shots are usual – better use No. 5. On a normal rise over dogs and for all around use, No. 6 is the favorite.
Grouse or Partridge	5, 6, 7 1/2, 8	Improved Cylinder or Modified – For Brush Work; Full – For Open Ranges	On the smaller birds such as ruffed grouse or Hungarian Partridge, use the smaller shot. The big western grouse (sage, sooty, and blue) call for heavier loads and larger shot.
Quail	7 1/2, 8, 9	Improved Cylinder or Modified	For early season shooting on bobwhites when feathers are light, some hunters use No. 9 shot. Later they switch to No. 7 1/2 or No. 8. On the running or wild flushing type of quail, such as the Gambel's, larger shot is sometimes used.
Doves and Pigeons	6, 7 1/2, 8, 9	Modified Improved Cylinder or Cylinder	Use lighter loads and No.7 1/2 or No. 8 shot on mourning doves at normal ranges – but for longer ranges use the heavy loads and No. 6 or No. 7 1/2. Use the same load on band-tailed pigeons and white wings.
Woodcock	7 1/2, 8, 9	Improved Cylinder or Modified	The choice of shot size here will depend on ranges at which the game is shot. For fast shooting in the alder thickets, No. 8 shot is a good choice.
Rabbits	4, 5, 6	Improved Cylinder or Modified – For Brush; Full – For Long Open Shots	For cottontail rabbits at normal range, the lighter loads are suitable, but for larger game such as jack rabbits and snow shoe rabbits use heavy loads.
Squirrels	5, 6	Modified	Most hunters use 5s or 6s and prefer the heavy loads particularly in the tall timber.
Rail	7 1/2, 8, 9	Improved Cylinder	For the little sora rail No. 8 or No. 9 does the job while many hunters use No. 7 1/2 on the marsh hen or clapper rail.
Turkey	BB, 2, 4, 5, 6, 7 1/2 ,	Full	Choice of shot size depends on the range. If you're a good caller, No. 6 or No. 7 1/2 shot makes a clean kill. BBs, No. 2, 4s, and 5s are best for long shots.

Game	Suggested Shot Size	Suggested Chokes	What Experienced Shotgunners Say...
Fox	BB, 2	Full	No. 2 shot is generally large enough and yet throws a fairly dense pattern.
Trap	7 1/2, 8	Full, Improved Modified, or Modified	In most cases, No. 7 1/2 is used for trap. Check the Official Rulebook.
Skeet	8,9	Skeet Choke, Improved Cylinder	In most cases, No. 9 is used for skeet. Check the Official Rulebook.
Hand Trap (or manual mechanical trap)	9, 8, 7 1/2	Any Choice (Depends on Practice Desired)	For targets at close range use a more open choke; at longer distances tighten the chokes.

HANDLOADING YOUR OWN

If you shoot a lot, you may want to consider handloading ammunition to save money and to increase the satisfaction you get from shotgun shooting. Handloading can serve both purposes and also be an interesting and fun hobby in itself. There are many different types of handloading equipment on the market today – from the simple and inexpensive to the complex and costly. Whichever you choose, be sure you follow manufacturer specifications for its operation and the use of ammunition components. Attending an NRA Shotgun Shell Reloading Course is recommended.

Shotshell reloading is an enjoyable and challenging hobby

3. SELECTING A SHOTGUN

In today's economy, any purchase of substance needs to be carefully thought out and wisely pursued. If you decide to purchase a shotgun, the same maxim holds here.

Your selection will depend on a number of variables – barrel lengths, different types of actions, gauge sizes; and gun fit. Balance and handling qualities will vary from model to model. Your job will involve delving through these many variables to come up with a combination that works best for you and your particular interests. Fortunately, ample help is available.

DO YOUR HOMEWORK

A trip to the local library can be time well spent in weeding out the types and applications not befitting your needs. Many fine books and articles have been published on the shotgun and its various uses. In them, you will find additional information that will help you make a wise choice. Gun manufacturers, not surprisingly, also go out of their way to acquaint you with their products and uses. The catalogs they publish are both illustrative and quite informative with regard to the various features available. You would do well to explore several of them.

If you are a NRA member you can receive the *American Rifleman*, *American Hunter*, or *America's 1ST Freedom*, three of several outstanding NRA magazines with many regular shotgunning articles. For ease in locating subjects of interest, each December issue of the *Rifleman* carries an index of the year's articles, topics and authors.

NRA publications
are an excellent
source of
shotgun information

CHECK WITH THE SPECIALISTS

Your local gun specialty store or sporting goods dealer should be able to provide you with a wealth of information. Gun dealers are often avid shooters themselves and are frequently aware of the various shooting organizations and events in your community. Time spent with them can be very productive.

Your local gun dealer can give guidelines on shotgun types, models and their merits

You might also consider taking a trip to your local gun club. Here, you'll find a host of shooting enthusiasts, who should be willing to sit down with you and share their experiences and recommendations. The more you pursue the sport, the more you'll discover that shooters tend to be both opinionated and genuinely committed to helping new participants in their chosen pastime. Shooting is a sport for participants, and the thrill is contagious.

ASK A FRIEND

If you happen to know someone who is a NRA member or active in shooting, his knowledge of firearms can be invaluable. He's not only looking at you as someone who shares his interests, he may also be welcoming you as a potential shooting companion! What's more, you won't need to feel shy in asking simple questions. Your friend will understand. He was once there, too.

19

CHECK THE REGULATIONS

Buying a shotgun with knowledge of the applicable gun laws in your community or state is just good common sense. Firearms laws affecting the purchase, as well as the ownership, possession, uses and carrying of firearms vary from state to state and from county to county. It's not only your legal obligation and responsibility to be aware of those pertaining to your locale, it's your duty to know them.

SOME THOUGHTS ON GUN FIT

There has been a great deal written on the subject of gun fit in years past. Most of it was intended for the average shooter. However, some technical information is really of use only to the professional stockmaker. The main point you should keep in mind when selecting a shotgun is that the majority of models manufactured today have standard stock dimensions designed to fit the average-sized adult. And, in most cases, they do. In addition, many manufacturers produce youth models of varying dimensions suitable to a youngster's physique.

Generally speaking, the most important consideration for fit is the length of the stock. With youngsters, people with short arms or small stature, a stock is often too long. The solution is simple. Cut it down to an appropriate size. It is best to have this done by a competent gunsmith who has experience in fitting stocks. On the other hand, if the stock appears to be too short, you can simply add a slip-on pad or spacer plates to lengthen it.

There are several tests to determine proper stock length, but the best guides are probably comfort and what you see. If you

If the shotgun fits, this is the view you should get when looking down the barrel

This youngster has a shotgun that was specifically designed and manufactured for young people. Trying to use dad's shotgun (left) just doesn't work

have done your homework well and have spent some time on the range with friends and instructor trying different guns, you should have a pretty good idea what feels comfortable. Second, when you place the stock to your face, you should be looking directly down the barrel. A good way to test this is to close your eyes and bring the gun into position and then open your eyes – your dominant eye should be aligned properly with the barrel.

WHICH GAUGE?

Some careful thought should be given to this subject. All too often people tend to think that a good beginner's shotgun is a .410, particularly for youngsters. But in fact, the .410 is a shot-

21

gun for the expert, not a beginner, and the reason is simple. The .410 places a much smaller number of shot in the air, thus reducing the likelihood for success. In shotgunning, the achievement of immediate success for the beginner is the key to establishing confidence in his ability and the fundamentals. Therefore, a 20 or 12 gauge shotgun is a better choice.

GAUGE COMPARISONS

Gauge	10	12	16	20	28	.410
Ounces of Shot in Standard Load	$1^5/_8$	$1^1/_8$	1	$^7/_8$	$^3/_8$	$^1/_2$
Quantity of Shot	951	658	585	512	439	292

Beginners often worry about the shotgun's recoil. But with a properly fitting gun and adherence to the fundamentals of shotgunning, recoil should be negligible factor in hitting the target.

▉ 4. SAFETY – YOUR RESPONSIBILITY

Managing you gun is your job, and your *attitude* must always be one of keeping total control over your firearm. It's not enough just to know the rules of safety. You must always maintain a *positive attitude* towards using them.

The basic safety rules fall in two categories: those you must observe whenever you are handling your shotgun and those required in the act of shooting.

RULES FOR SAFE GUN HANDLING

The fundamental NRA rules for the safe gun handling are:

1. ALWAYS keep the gun pointed in a safe direction. This is the primary rule of gun safety. A safe direction means that the gun is pointed so that even if it were to go off it would not cause injury or damage. The key to this rule is to control where the muzzle or front end of the barrel is pointed at all times. Common sense dictates the safest direction, depending on the different circumstances.

2. _ALWAYS_ keep your finger off the trigger until ready to shoot. When holding a gun, rest your trigger finger outside the trigger guard alongside the gun. Until you are actually ready to fire, do not touch the trigger.

3. _ALWAYS_ keep the gun unloaded until ready to use. Whenever you pick up a gun, always keep the gun pointed in a safe direction, keep your finger off the trigger, engage the mechanical safety if possible, remove the ammunition source (magazine or ammunition from the magazine tube), open the action, visually and physically inspect the chamber(s) and magazine area, which should be clear of ammunition and leave the action open with the mechanical safety engaged. If you do not know how to open the action or inspect the chamber(s) leave the gun alone and get help from someone who does.

Always keep the gun pointed in a safe direction

Always keep your finger off the trigger until ready to shoot

Always keep the gun unloaded until ready to use

RULES FOR SAFE SHOOTING

When using or storing a gun, always follow these NRA rules:

• ***Know your target and what is beyond.*** Be absolutely sure you have identified your target beyond any doubt. Equally important, be aware of the area beyond your target. This means observing your prospective area of fire before you shoot. Never fire in a direction in which there are people or any other potential for mishap. Think first. Shoot second. (The maximum range of No. 9 lead pellets loaded in a standard cartridge is almost 700 feet. No. 00 pellets have a maximum range of approximately 1,830 feet, and 12 gauge shotgun slugs have a range of approximately 2,450 feet).

• ***Know how to use the gun safely.*** Before handling a gun, learn how it operates. Know it's basic parts, how to safely open and close the action, and how to remove any ammunition from the gun or magazine. Remember, a gun's mechanical safety device is never foolproof. Nothing can ever replace safe gun handling.

• ***Be sure the gun is safe to operate.*** Just like other tools, guns need regular maintenance to remain operable. Regular cleaning and proper storage are part of the gun's general upkeep. If there is any question concerning a gun's ability to function, a knowledgeable gunsmith should look at it.

• ***Use only the correct ammunition for your gun.*** Only the cartridges or shells designed for a particular gun can be fired safely in that gun. Most guns have the ammunition type stamped on the barrel. Ammunition can be identified by information printed on the box and sometimes stamped on the cartridge. Do not shoot the gun unless you know you have the proper ammunition.

As a safety measure, be sure to carry only one gauge or caliber of ammunition. It may be possible to accidentally insert a small shell of the wrong gauge or caliber into the chamber of a gun that requires a larger gauge or caliber. In such cases, the small shell can slide forward into the barrel, forming an obstruction. If a larger shell is then loaded into the chamber behind the smaller shell and the gun is fired, this obstruction (and possible ignition of the smaller shell) can cause severe damage to the gun and serious injury to the shooter.

• *Wear eye and ear protection as appropriate.* Guns are loud and the noise can cause hearing damage. They can also emit debris and hot gas that could cause eye injury. For these reasons, shooting glasses and hearing protectors should be worn by shooters and spectators.

• *Never use alcohol or drugs before or while shooting.* Alcohol, as well as any other substances likely to impair normal mental or physical bodily functions, must not be used before or while handling or shooting guns. Even the over-the-counter (non-prescription) medications, such as cold remedies, allergy medicines, and cough syrups, can impair judgment and cause undesirable physical side effects. These side effects can include loss of concentration, vision problems, shakiness, and drowsiness and could result in an accident.

• *Store guns so they are not accessible to unauthorized persons.* Several factors should be considered when you decide on where and how you intend to store your guns.

Wear ear and eye protection

25

Your particular situation will be a major part of the consideration. Safe and secure storage requires that untrained individuals (especially children) be denied access to your guns.

• **Be aware that certain types of guns and many shooting activities require additional safety precautions.** The safety precautions needed for all types of guns and shooting activities are too numerous to list here. You may need to follow additional safety rules, regulations, and instructions for your type of gun and shooting activity. Shooting ranges, for examples, usually have special range rules that must be followed by all shooters.

Your club's range officer can help you have a safe and more enjoyable shooting experience.

5. CARING FOR YOUR SHOTGUN

Your shotgun has been built to last. And, with your help, it will. The cleaning and maintenance chores required to keep your gun in tip-top shape are relatively simple and require little time or effort. They must, however, be undertaken with regularity to safeguard against deterioration and assure continued proper functioning.

Cleaning is important for a shotgun. Every time you shoot it, a minor fire breaks out inside the shotgun. Firing leaves a sooty residue which can foul moving parts, the bore and chamber, and produce inefficient – even unsafe – shooting conditions.

Since firearms are largely made of metal, rust is also an ever-present danger. Safeguarding against corrosion through regular cleaning and lubrication will add many years to the life of your shotgun.

Some forethought must be also applied to questions concerning the proper storage and transportation of your shotgun.

CLEANING AND MAINTAINING YOUR SHOTGUN

Regular cleaning is not only important, but can be fun. Here's a basic guide to follow. But first, two considerations should be addressed.

How often should you clean your gun? Ideally, the answer should be after each day of use. This may not always be practical, but one precaution is mandatory. No shotgun should be fired without prior cleaning after prolonged storage. Otherwise, accumulated moisture or dirt could affect the gun's performance, and could even be hazardous.

What special tools and supplies will be needed? Check the owner's manual that accompanies your gun to determine the specific materials and procedures required for cleaning. Generally, however, you will need:

- *Cleaning Rod with Attachments.* This allows you to reach inside the barrel to remove dirt and residue. Attachments usually include a cloth swab, patch holder and brush that fits the bore.

A cleaning kit should include cleaning rod attachments, cleaning patches, bore solvent, brush, gun oil and a clean cloth

- **Cleaning Patches.** These fabrics, available commercially or made at home from absorbent cloth, allow you to remove foreign particles form the barrel's interior surface and to apply solvent or lubricant as well.

- **Bore Cleaning Solvent.** The bore generally collects more debris than any other part of your gun. This residue can be removed through the use of several commercially available cleaning agents.

- **Light Gun Oil.** The metallic components, including the moving parts, of your gun may require lubrication to function efficiently. Again, check the manufacturer's recommendations. A good grade of gun oil, available from any gun dealer, should be used for this purpose.

- **Clean Cloth.** The exterior surfaces of your shotgun cannot be overlooked. Have a cloth that is free of dirt and moisture available for wiping down.

- **Small Brush.** This item is handy for cleaning the inaccessible nooks and crannies on your gun. An old toothbrush serves this purpose well.

Shown on the following pages are some of the things that you should do to keep your shotgun in proper condition. (Note: Some bore cleaners may require applications techniques that are different from those described below. Always use bore cleaners according to the manufacturer's instructions.

IMPORTANT!! Before starting to clean your gun **be absolutely certain** that it is unloaded and the action is open.

- Moisten a cloth patch with bore cleaner and use a patch-holder tip to run it through the entire length of the bore several times.

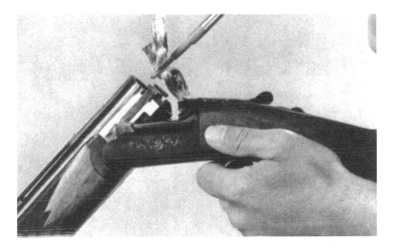

- Next run a dry patch through the bore. If the patch comes out dirty, clean the bore again with a patch moistened with bore cleaner. Run another dry patch through the bore. If the patch comes out dirty again, repeat these cleaning steps until a dry patch comes out clean. (If the bore is very dirty, you may need to remove the patch-holder tip and substitute a cleaning brush that has been moistened with bore cleaner. After using the brush, re-attach the patch-holder tip; clean the bore using moistened and dry patches as described above.) Finally, run a lightly-oiled patch through the bore to prevent rust.

- Wipe all the exterior surfaces of your shotgun with a clean cloth, being particularly careful to remove any accumulated grease or dirt form the gun's moving parts. A small brush may be useful.

- Check all the removable parts of your gun – including the stock, screws, magazine, tube cap and similar parts – to be sure they are fastened tightly.

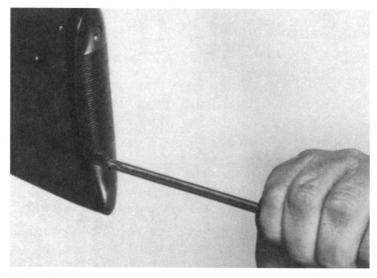

- Wipe the metal surfaces of the shotgun with a lightly-oiled soft rag or a silicone -impregnated cloth.

GUN REPAIRS

You should not attempt to repair any part of your shotgun that appears to be malfunctioning or broken. At this point in your shooting career even the most minor repairs should be left to an expert. There's a simple reason for this. With minimal knowledge, any improper repair could cause the gun to fire improperly or cause further damage – with potentially hazardous results. At minimum, you could irreparably damage your firearm. Don't take chances. Take your shotgun to an experienced gunsmith and let him solve the problem for you.

TRANSPORTING YOUR SHOTGUN

The complex legal requirements associated with firearm usage are a particular consideration when you prepare to transport your shotgun. Since applicable state and local regulations vary a great deal, you must make it your business to know what the laws say at home, at points in transit and at your destination. Some localities have ordinances restricting firearm transport. Others are more reasonable. In any case, knowing and complying with the laws are part of your obligations as a responsible shooter.

Most states permit you to legally transport firearms if they are unloaded, cased and locked in the trunk of your car. You may also consider separating your shotgun form it's ammunition as an additional precaution.

Proper care during transporting will maintain the beauty of your shotgun

SENSIBLE STORAGE

Several factors should be considered when you decide on where, and how, you intend to store your shotgun. Your particular needs will be a major part of the consideration. So will the storage capabilities of your dwelling. Safety and security must also be contemplated rationally. The storage of a shotgun requires the exercise of ordinary care after viewing all the circumstances.

Bear this in mind when making your decision. Firearms are attractive items for people to handle. You have to make the assumption that an untrained person attempting to handle your gun may not do so safely. Consequently, it could be in your interest and that of your guest as well, to store your gun in a place that does not afford ready access to small children, or to the neophyte adult. Many fine wooden cases are presently available for purchase which not only store firearms with a measure of security but also display them to attractive advantage. Some shooters who desire even more secure storage capability keep their guns in metal vaults. Others who do not have such facilities elect to lock their guns away, with the keys kept in a place where they are not likely to be found by youngsters or casual visitors.

Proper storage can also allow you to enjoy your firearms while at home

Shotguns kept in storage should be unloaded. And when you are removing your gun from its storage place, make it your first order of business to open the action and be sure no shell had been errantly left in the chamber or magazine.

Proper attention should also be devoted to storing your ammunition. Your shells should be kept in a cool, dry place. In most cases it's wise to keep shells and guns stored separately.

PART TWO:
BASIC
SHOOTING
SKILLS

▉ 1. THE FUNDAMENTALS OF SHOTGUN SHOOTING

Learning to shoot is like mastering any other skill. No first-day skier of sound mind would venture to the top of the peak for his very first run. Nor should you, as a first-time shooter, begin your expedition by loading up and blasting away at targets flying every which direction. Your introduction to shotgun shooting must start with an appreciation of what must be accomplished in the process of learning and using basic skills required to hit a moving target.

Accordingly, we begin our instructions with a discussion of the *fundamentals of shotgun shooting.* Five steps are involved here. We refer to them as "fundamentals" because they must be practiced and adhered to in exact sequence each and every time you take a shot. Once you've learned the fundamentals, you can begin to apply them in a variety of shotgunning sports.

The five fundamentals are:

1. stance

2. gun ready position

3. swing to target

4. trigger pull

5. follow through

Before you start learning these fundamentals, there's an important question you must answer for yourself. On which side should you shoulder the gun? The answer isn't as obvious as it may seem. Just because you may be right-handed doesn't mean that your right side is best for firing. The true test is whether your right or left *eye* is "dominant".

You may not be conscious of it, but if you're like most people you probably have one eye that is more dominant than the other. Since the ability to align the shotgun with a moving target is so essential, you should use your "dominant" eye and shoulder your gun on that side. But how do you determine which eye is dominant? There's an easy test:

- Extend your hands in front of your face, placing them together so that only a small opening remains between them. Now look through this space, focusing of some distant object with both eyes open.

- While maintaining your focus, keep both eyes open and start slowly moving your hands closer to your face. Continue this motion until your hands reach the face. At this point, you will have instinctively lined the opening in your hands up with a single eye. That's your dominant eye!

Now that you have this information you should learn and practice the fundamentals accordingly.

STANCE

Stance is the position of your body in the act of shooting and its relationship to the expected target. Two conditions are essential for a good stance. First, your stance must be comfortable and relaxed. This means attaining as natural balance as possible without straining your muscles. Imagine yourself in a basic boxing position. Your feet should be about shoulder width apart and planted firmly on the ground. Your front knee should be bent forward slightly while your back leg remains straight. If you have trouble grasping this idea, study the boxer's position in the illustration. In shotgun shooting, you're seeking the same position because it provides proper balance and the ability to move. Aligning your stance with the expected target breaking area is the second essential condition. This will permit you to easily rotate your body if the target moves to the left or right.

A good shooting stance is very similar to the basic stance of a boxer (left). With slight adjustment of the hand and arm (middle), the shotgun can be added for a correct shooting position (right)

Line up stance with expected target breaking area (left)

With a shotgun added, you can move quickly to the target (right)

GUN READY POSITION

The gun ready position is the posture you assume before actually moving your gun to shoot the target. It is intended to make your subsequent "swing to the target" as easy as possible. Maintaining your basic shooting stance, you should hold the shotgun with your non-trigger hand at about the middle of the shotgun forearm. Your grip should be just firm enough to provide control, but not so firm as to create unnecessary strain. The same is true of the trigger hand placed on the grip of the stock.

A gun ready position is relaxed and enhances your ability to see the target area

Place the muzzle just below the anticipated target's flight path to allow a clear view of target – keep both eyes open

The rear position of the stock is positioned along the front side of your ribs. The muzzle is placed slightly below the expected flight path of your target, thus providing you a clear view of the target area., Both your eyes should remain open, and focused in the area where you expect your target will first appear.

41

SWING TO TARGET

On first seeing the target, move your gun and body as a single coordinated unit toward the target while raising the gun into the correct firing position. To achieve this position:

- Keep your eyes focused on the target all the time.
- Bring the stock to the face. It should be firmly in place against the cheek.
- The trigger hand elbow comes into position about level with the shoulders.
- Place the butt of the stock against the shoulder.

With correct gun fit, the barrel will be aligned in front of your dominant eye and with the target. The swing to target must all be done quickly, but in a smooth and fluid movement.

A good shooting position – **study it!**

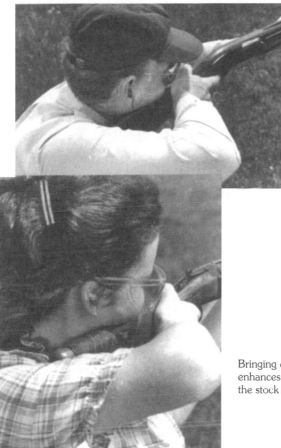

Keep comb of stock firmly in position against cheek of face

Bringing elbow to shoulder level enhances proper positioning of the stock against shoulder and face

We don't like to show the wrong ways but will this time to make a point! Leaving the elbow down allows only a small portion of the butt to contact the shoulder, causing, among other problems, discomfort and bruising during firing

43

TRIGGER PULL

Timing and reflex are essential in the act of trigger pull. The trigger pull should take place at the instant when, looking at the moving target, you see the gun's muzzle touch it. Your trigger pull must be crisp and quick.

FOLLOW THROUGH

Follow through is one of the most important and most difficult aspects of shotgun shooting. The shotgun muzzle must move through the target if the shots are to hit the target. The trigger is pulled while the shotgun is moving, and the gun must continue to move after the shot is fired. The shotgun must remain "welded" to the body, especially the cheek. Stopping the motion of the shotgun on touching the target is probably the most common cause of misses by beginning shotgunners. Always continue to *keep the gun moving by following through!*

Knowing the fundamentals is the foundation of successful shooting. Using them correctly each and *every* time *consistently* provides successful shooting, whether you're a beginner or an expert. As you're about to discover, the steps involved in commencing actual shooting are methodical, progressive and equally vital.

Follow through is essential to consistent success. Continue to do the same thing immediately after, as you did before, the shot

2. FIRING YOUR FIRST SHOTS

Now that you know how your shotgun operates, how to care for and use it safely, and the fundamentals upon which successful shooting is structured, you're ready to begin working up to your first shots. This is a multi-step process and the most effective way to produce the desired results is to be patient and take it a step at a time. Only after proper preparation and review is the shotgun, and then ammunition, added. The rewards will come when you find your shots hitting the target rather than thin air.

KNOW YOUR TARGET

In the exercises to come, you will be building up to your first shots firing on airborne targets thrown by hand or a mechanical "trap". But first, you'll need to know the target itself.

An inexpensive mechanical or hand trap can provide hundreds of hours of productive practice

The breakable "clay target" is excellent for learning, and is used by the millions in target competition. Clay targets are readily available at most sporting goods stores. Some gun clubs and ranges may provide them for their participants. They are easily thrown with an inexpensive manual trap, and cost very little themselves.

Learn everything you can about the target. Handle it and see how easily it breaks. Observe how its design facilitates flight much like a frisbee. Then watch several of them in flight. On the range, you will notify the trap operator that you want a target thrown with the command, "pull". Notice how the target moves out from the trap when it is ejected. Get a feel for how fast and where the target flies.

With this knowledge, you're ready to prepare for your first shots.

The first step to successful shooting is to become familiar with the target's flight. Know what to expect!

START WITH STRAIGHTAWAY TARGET

Accomplished hunters, trap and skeet shooters fire from a number of positions and with targets coming or going from many directions, angles, speeds and distances. But at the outset, you should practice on targets flying in only one basic direction. Here, the trap is set so that it will throw the target fairly straightaway in front of you. Initially, each target should follow virtually the same

Beginners learning on a regulation trap field should shoot from a position immediately behind the trap house

flight path and travel at a relatively slow speed. The background against which the target will be thrown should be clear – an open sky with a low horizon line and no obstructions is ideal. All of this enhances your ability to concentrate and focus on the target – and hit it.

On a skeet field, the best place to start is on station 7 with a straightaway low house target

LEARN TO POINT

Before you actually start working with your shotgun, it's advisable to grow accustomed to running through the shooting fundamentals with a target – but with your index finger substituting for the shotgun itself. This exercise will teach you to point toward the flying target without having to concentrate at the same time on the necessary body movements required to position the shotgun. This will also enhance your ability to *concentrate on the target* at all times.

Assume the basic "boxer" stance, but with your index finger pointed at a 45 degree angle to the ground as illustrated. Remember, line up your stance with the expected target breaking area. If your right eye is dominant, point with your left hand finger. If it's your left eye, point with the right hand finger. By doing this, when the time comes to add your shotgun, your stance will be correct. Now, focus your eyes on the area where your target will first appear and call "pull".

47

Assume this position before you call "PULL" to receive the target

Pointing with your finger is the same thing you'll do with a shotgun – "POINT" it

As soon as you see your target, immediately and smoothly move your finger to the target and keep your finger aligned with it until it hits the ground. Practice this motion several times. Notice …you looked at the target all the time, not the finger you were pointing with. This is an important concept in shotgun shooting – shotguns are pointed, not aimed. The difference – your eyes must always remain focused on the target, never the shotgun barrel or beads. When you begin to feel comfortable with this pointing exercise, add a sound effect.

Notice when pointing at a target with your finger, you always watch the target – the same thing should be true when you point with your shotgun

When the target is released, again move your finger to it smoothly. At the instant your finger "touches" the target, simulate pulling the trigger by saying "BANG!" Remember to follow through. This may sound a bit too much like kid's stuff for your tastes, but there's a distinct purpose in this. In shotgun shooting, it is imperative to be able to time your shot so that you pull the trigger as soon as the muzzle touches the target. By calling "BANG", you are learning to recognize and develop a mental picture of actions in shooting that should eventually become instinctive.

PRACTICE POINTING WITH YOUR SHOTGUN

Now you can pick up your shotgun. Before doing so, however, remember the basic safety rules. Keep your muzzle pointed in a safe direction at all times and keep your finger off the trigger until you're ready to shoot. Check to make sure both the chamber and magazine are unloaded by opening the action and ascertaining that no shells remain inside.

Your first actions with the shotgun in your hands should be to complete a total review of the first three shooting fundamentals without a target. Get into the proper stance. Make sure your stance is balanced and allows you to rotate easily to the left and right of the planned shooting area. Assume the gun ready position. Now practice bringing the shotgun from the gun ready position into the correct firing position. Check to be sure you're doing every fundamental "according to the book". Take your time – practice. Once you've learned to bring the shotgun smoothly into the correct firing position from the gun ready position, it's time to add the target.

Practice calling for and swinging to the target following it all the way to the ground. This teaches you to stay with your gun. Be sure your eyes remain focused on the target all the time.

DRY-FIRING

After working on the first three fundamentals, you can add pulling the trigger – with the gun action closed but unloaded. This is called dry-firing. After checking the chamber and magazine close the action, place the safety in the "off" position and assume your stance and gun ready position. Now call "pull" – this time pulling the trigger the instant your muzzle touches the target.

Before actually attempting your first shot, practice the fundamentals over and over (dry firing) until you can do them smoothly and correctly

Now's the time to really work on the follow through. Doing everything exactly the same as you did the instant you pulled the trigger, practice staying with the gun two to three seconds after firing. Remember, continue to keep the stock firmly in place against the cheek. Open the action after each shot, as if you were ejecting a spent shell.

SHOOTING LIVE AMMUNITION

After you have dry-fired a number of times and are confident in your ability to successfully perform all the shooting fundamentals, you are now ready to begin shooting with ammunition. However, you will need to return your gun to the rack to get prepared. Start with a review of all the firearm handling and shooting rules. Make sure you know them – and follow them! Next, put on your eye and ear protectors. Get yourself no more than five rounds of ammunition, pick up your shotgun and you're ready to move to the firing station. From here on it's a good idea to learn to do each step by the numbers. Learning to do the steps the same way each and every time is the key to "consistent" success in shooting. Follow the seven steps listed below:

1. Move to station, load appropriate number of shell(s) (in this case, just one) and place gun's safety in "off" position.
2. Establish stance in relation to the target-breaking area.

3. Establish *gun ready position* with muzzle slightly below target flight path and place finger on trigger.
4. Focus eyes in the area where target will soon appear.
5. Call "PULL" for target.
6. On seeing target, swing to target, *pull trigger* and *follow through*.
7. Open action and unload shotgun immediately after firing.

If you have done everything right, remembering to follow through, you should have a broken target.

How did you do? If you followed the fundamentals you should have broken a target. If not, don't be too hard on yourself if your untouched target dropped to the ground. This is just the beginning of many eventful days of shooting to come. As in all sports requiring skill and coordination, successful shotgun shooting means ongoing practice. So try again! As you refine your ability to concentrate on the target, you'll begin to see targets breaking one after the other!

The first broken target – an exiting and memorable occasion

You'll want to practice with straightaway targets for several sessions, until you hit them fairly consistently. Then you can move on to more difficult targets by gradually changing their angles of flight.

3. MOVING ON – ADVANCED SHOOTING SKILLS

Up to now, you have been shooting fairly straightaway targets. As pointed out in the foreword, you should learn the simple skills before moving on the more complex ones. Straightaway targets were hopefully easier to hit, but not just because they were straightaway. Among several things that made them seem easier were that you knew in advance where they were going and what to expect. Also, in the previous exercises, many of the variables normally associated with more advanced shooting were carefully controlled for you and, where possible, eliminated. The reason was to help you focus your attention (concentration) on one thing – the target. Therefore, as much as possible, the exercise guaranteed the success of your first attempt at shooting moving targets – building your confidence, as well as, your skills.

Field targets are unpredictable and are a good test of shotgunning skills

If you have progressed according to the book, it is now time to move on to more "complex" or advanced targets. What are some of the variables that make them difficult?

Under various conditions, targets can come from the right or the left of the shooter, from a position in which the target flies toward or away from the shooter, and at various speeds, altitudes and angles. In addition, in some cases you may receive more than one target at the same time and not know the direction of flight or the exact moment of release.

The combinations are endless. However, all these variables do not change the fundamentals you've just learned. Even though the targets and their flights may change, the fundamentals don't! They are the foundation on which all shotgun shooting is built. But to use the fundamentals successfully on various targets, you'll need additional knowledge and understanding of the overall shooting process. As you begin to study and talk to others, you will find there are several different methods used for shooting moving targets. Of these, we have chosen to focus on the "swing through" method. This method offers the simplest and fastest road to progress and provides a wider base for overall development of your skills. The name of the method is derived form the fact that you actually swing through the target. This is done by simply coming up behind and accelerating through the target. Again, firing as the barrel touches the target in passing. It's important that you understand how this method works.

The key lies in understanding the series of time delays which occur in the shooting process. The first time delay is human reaction, the brief span of time between the brain's decision to fire and the actual pulling of the trigger. The second delay is a mechanical delay, the time it takes the firing mechanism to function from the trigger pull to the muzzle blast. The third and last delay is the time it takes for the shot charge to reach the target. Though collectively these delays occur in what appears to be a negligible instant, what you are doing during the instant they occur can make the difference between hitting or missing the target. Although all fundamentals are important in hitting a target, in this method firing at the right time and a strong follow through are essential keys to consistent success.

The follow through takes care of what is often referred to as the lead. Lead is simply the distance between the target and muzzle at the time of the firing. In the swing through method, measuring lead, as required in the other methods, is not necessary because it is automatically taken care of when the shooting method is executed properly. Not having to do this measuring allows you to concentrate on the target and not on the figuring and measuring of the distance between the target and an abstract point.

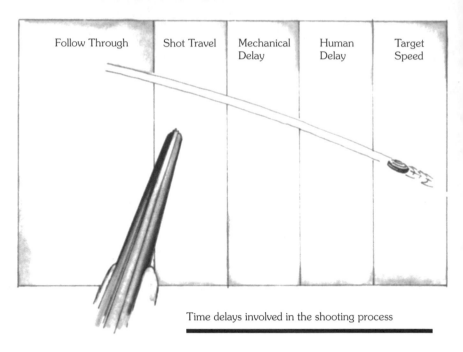

Follow Through	Shot Travel	Mechanical Delay	Human Delay	Target Speed

Time delays involved in the shooting process

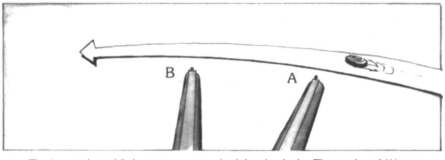

The "swing through" shooter gives more lead than he thinks. The gun barrel (A) shows where he thinks he shoots on a crossing target. The barrel (B) is where he really shoots if a good follow through is used

Remember, while swinging to the target, shooting at the target and following through – keep the gun moving all the time.

Having learned the fundamentals, before too long you'll want to seek out shooting opportunities that accommodate your growing interests. That's when the excitement really begins!

PART THREE:
*LOOK
AT THE
OPPORTUNITIES*

■ 1. SHOOTING – A SKILL THAT LASTS A LIFETIME

Equipped with your new knowledge and skills, as well as with a commitment to develop them, you are becoming a shotgun shooter. You have joined an outstanding group of shooting participants. Throughout the world, the men and women who practice shotgun shooting in its various forms number in the millions. And the list of activities designed to meet the diverse interests of this enormous group is equally impressive.

Difference in ages and backgrounds of shooters only seems to enhance the fun of it all

Having grasped the basics of effective shotgun shooting, your next order of business will undoubtedly be to build upon this foundation of knowledge and skill, and to begin to channel your interests in specific directions. Perhaps your goals lie in hunting. Hunting with a shotgun is one of America's most popular forms of recreation, with millions of licenses issued every year. A wide range of competitive shotgun shooting events are available, geared to every level of ability, and are organized at the local, state, national and international levels. And on a less formal basis, an easy-going day spent outdoors with friends and a hand trap can be a most gratifying experience.

If you're like most new shooters, you'll want to develop your skills as quickly and thoroughly as possible. That's an enviable goal, but be forewarned: Try as you might, you're not going to become an expert shot overnight. Proficiency in shotgunning, like any other skill, is a lengthy process. It takes hours of dedicated practice. The rewards come in being able to see tangible improvements each time you go shooting. There's always something new to learn, some improvement in technique to work out, some new challenge to pursue. And that, in a nutshell, is the joy of the shooting experience: the eternal presence of yet another plateau to scale, and the constant realization of rewards for a job well done.

Fortunately, you won't have to become an "expert" marksman to begin enjoying the lion's share of the shooting activities available to you now. They're at your disposal – right now. And so is a vast array of dedicated shooters from every walk of life, in whose company you will find the sport more challenging, more diverse and, quite simply, more fun.

TRAINING

This manual has been designed to give you the basic tools required for learning the various skills of shotgun shooting. It cannot, however, provide one valuable learning component: feedback. It's much easier to acquire good habits than to break bad ones. One of the quickest and most effective ways of learning to shoot properly is to have an expert teach you. You can get that level of expert guidance by enrolling in a NRA Basic Shotgun Shooting Course.

Throughout America, thousands of National Rifle Association Certified Shotgun Instructors offer these courses for new shooters each year. NRA's Training Department can put you in touch with an NRA Certified Instructor in your area.

You may also want to look into attending some of the gunsmithing courses offered by one for the many NRA Short-Term Gunsmithing Schools. These schools are located in various parts of the country, and have short-term courses that range form one day to two weeks in length. Course offerings vary from year to year. For information about these schools, contact NRA's Education and Training Division. (Also see Appendix 5 in this book for additional information.)

You can get recognition awards and skill growth through the Winchester/ NRA Marksmanship Qualification Course

QUALIFICATION SHOOTING

You can develop and improve your shooting skills by participating in the Winchester/NRA Shotgun Qualification Course. In this course, shooters are required to achieve certain minimum scores on NRA-designated courses of fire. Advancing at their own pace, shooters are rewarded with a patch, rockers, medals, pins and certificates. After meeting the criteria for an award level, shooters advance to the next level. (A copy of this course is printed as an appendix in this book.) The NRA Sport Shooting Qualifications Courses also contain various shotgun courses of fire. For information, contact the Winchester/NRA's Marksmanship Qualification Program Coordinator in the Education and Training Division.

Whether you wish to compete or not, the games of skeet and trap shooting are a great way of advancing your shotgunning skills

COMPETITION

Even if you have no particular ambition to excel in prestigious shotgun tournaments, you could well find participation in formal shooting competition a valuable way of refining your abilities. The games of skeet, trap, and sporting clays shooting were originally designed for the purpose of enhancing hunting skills. Even though they have evolved into sports events with their own following, they still provide the best means for sharpening your shotgunning skills for the field. By testing your skills against others at your own level, you can learn by observing while experiencing the special thrill of competitive achievement. Sanctioned skeet, trap, and sporting clays shooting competitions provide just such an opportunity.

In sanctioned competitions, shooters compete according to ability level. After participating in a few matches, you'll be eligible to receive a national classification card that will identify your skill level. This card enables you to be grouped with shooters of similar skills should you wish to shoot competitively for awards at the local, state and national level. Contact the National Skeet Shooting Association, Amateur Trapshooting Association, and National Sporting Clays Association for more information on these programs.

HUNTING

The vast majority of shotgun shooters are hunters. Each year, nearly 20 million hunting licenses are purchased in the United States. Even if your primary interest is in clay target shooting, the natural appeal and camaraderie of taking your shotgun into

Millions of hunters enjoy the outdoors while pursuing their favorite game

the field with friends may catch up with you sooner or later.

There's a whole new element of shooting responsibility connected with hunting. A vast array of game birds and animals can be legally pursued with a shotgun. These activities are, however, regulated and subject to various laws. It will be your responsibility to know and observe those regulations and firearms laws pertaining to the species you intend to pursue. Your state Fish and Game Department or Wildlife Division can provide you with the necessary details or you can contact the NRA Hunter Services Department for additional information.

As a beginning hunter, you should enroll in the hunter safety education course offered by your state. Many states require completion of these courses as a prerequisite to issuing a hunting license. Even if this is not the case in your chosen hunting area, you'll find the course interesting, informative and an excellent introduction to the hunting experience. The NRA Hunter Service Department provides a wealth of information about hunting seasons, regulations, available clinics and other subjects of interest to the hunter. The NRA also publishes the American Hunter, a magazine designed especially for its hunting members.

■ 2. JOIN THE SHOOTING FELLOWSHIP!

Shooting isn't just a hobby. For many people, it's a major part of life. There's something about it that naturally draws people together. Perhaps it's because shooting is so much more fulfilling when pursued in the company of others who love it. Perhaps it's because the challenge of shooting is enhanced when skills are compared and tested. Perhaps it's because safety is advanced when several people shoot together and look out for each other's welfare. Over the years, shooting has evolved into a truly great American experience. From coast to coast, millions of men and women representing the whole spectrum of society have organized at the local, state and national level to pursue their shooting interests and promote the sport. You, too, will find that participation in one or several of the many shooting organizations available to you will be a valuable part of your shooting experience.

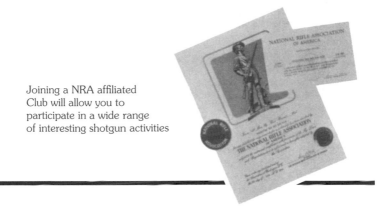

Joining a NRA affiliated
Club will allow you to
participate in a wide range
of interesting shotgun activities

LOCAL SHOOTING CLUBS

The local shooting club is the place where many new shooting activities and social opportunities are open to you. Through participation in one of the 15,000 local clubs affiliated with the NRA you'll find a readily accessible place to shoot. You'll also find NRA Certified Instructors to help you develop your skills. In addition, you'll have the opportunities to participate in qualification programs and in club competitions. But best of all, you'll find a host of fine folks who share your interests and desire your companionship.

You'll make many new friendships that will last a lifetime

The NRA Clubs and Associations Department can provide you with a list of shooting clubs in your area.

STATE SHOOTING ASSOCIATIONS

NRA-affiliated state associations exist to promote and support a wide range of shooting and related activities for gun owners and shooters. The success of shooting programs in your state depends, in large part, on your active involvement. Officers of your state association will be pleased to fill you in on the various programs and services they offer. The NRA Clubs and Associations Department can also put you in touch with them.

THE NATIONAL RIFLE ASSOCIATION OF AMERICA

NRA activities reach out to encompass virtually every element of the shooting world. Its programs range from activities involving gunsmithing and gun collecting to the development of America's competitive shooters. The NRA sanctions or sponsors competitions, tournaments, and shooting championships in communities across America. It sets national standards for training, safety, competition, coaching, shooting, and hunting. NRA members periodically receive magazines full of informative articles about shooting activities and events. They have opportunities to participate in attractive group insurance programs and other benefits. And they have access to a wide array of publications encompassing the whole spectrum of shooting and firearm interests. NRA is also foremost guardian of your constitutional right to own and use firearms for all legitimate purposes.

Your membership and active participation in the NRA will help support its vital programs. Whatever your interest in firearms and shooting, NRA encourages you to become part of the great and growing NRA family.

APPENDIXES

■ APPENDIX 1: WINCHESTER/NRA SHOTGUN QUALIFICATION COURSE

This qualification course may be fired on trap, skeet, or sporting clays ranges.

Award levels in this course consist of Pro-Marksman, Marksman, Marksman 1st Class, Sharpshooter, Expert, and Distinguished Expert.

Rules

- Awards may be earned by anyone.
- Awards must be earned in the following order: Promarksman, Marksman, Marksman 1st Class, Sharpshooter, Expert, and Distinguished Expert. Awards consist of a patch, rockers, medals, pins and certificates.
- Scores may be fired at any time, either in formal competition or in practice.
- Scores used to earn one award cannot be used again to earn another award.
- Any shotgun not larger than a 12 gauge may be used. The same gun need not be used for all rounds or for all qualification ratings earned.
- Standard rules for trap, skeet, or sporting clays must be used.
- The term round refers to a series of 25 targets.
- Rounds used for qualification need not be fired in sequence.
- Distinguished Expert qualifying rounds must be witnessed by an NRA member or NRA Instructor or Coach.
- Rules Sources:

  Skeet: National Skeet Shooting Association .... (800) 877-5338
  Trap: Amateur Trapshooting Association .... (937) 898-4638
  Sporting Clays: National Sporting Clays Assoc. ..... (800) 877-5338

- Rules of the Amateur Trapshooting Association, National Skeet Shooting Association, or National Sporting Clays Association apply.
- Program award levels and qualification scores.

SKEET OR TRAP

Award Levels	Number of 25 Target Rounds	Minimum Score Per Round
Pro-Marksman	2	11
Marksman	4	13
Marksman 1st Class	6	15
Sharpshooter	6	17
Expert	10	19
Distinguished Expert	10*	22

*or 84 or better out of 100 targets in two ATA or NSSA registered shoots.

SPORTING CLAYS

Award Levels	Number of Repetitions	Minimum Scores
Pro-Marksman	2	10 of 50
Marksman	4	16 of 50
Marksman 1st Class	4	20 of 50
Sharpshooter	5	22 of 50
Expert	3	52 of 100
Distinguished Expert	3**	60 of 100

** or 57 or better out of 100 targets in two NSCA registered shoots.

ORDERING QUALIFICATION COURSE MATERIALS & AWARDS

To place an order, contact the NRA Program Materials Center by telephoning (800) 336-7402 between 8:30 a.m. and 11:00 p.m. Weekdays, 10:00 a.m. and 6:00 p.m. Eastern Time Saturday and Sunday, or by writing to P.O. Box 5000, Kearneysville, West Virginia 25430-5000.

■■■■ **APPENDIX 2: NRA RESOURCES**

THE NRA IS HERE TO HELP – WE'RE AS NEAR AS THE TELEPHONE OR MAILBOX!

To contact the NRA for assistance or additional information, please direct all inquiries to:

> National Rifle Association of America
> 11250 Waples Mill Road
> Fairfax, VA. 22030
> Phone: (703) 267-1000
> (Main Switchboard)

For questions relating to specific NRA divisions, send mail inquiries directly to the attention of those divisions at the above address, or use the following telephone numbers:

Community Service Programs Division.... (703) 267-1560

Competitive Shooting Division .... (703) 267-1450

Education & Training Division.................. (703) 267-1500

Field Operations Division .... (703) 267-1340

General Counsel's Office .... (703) 267-1250

Institute for Legislative Action
Grassroots .... (703) 267-1170

Membership Division
All locations **except** Virginia.................... (800) NRA-3888
In Virginia.. (703) 267-3888

National Firearms Museum....................... (703) 267-1600

Other NRA resources can be contacted at the following addresses and phone numbers:

Club Liability Insurance
Lockton Risk Services
PO Box 410679
Kansas City, MO 64141-0679 .... (877) 487-5407

NRA Program Materials Center
NRA Program Materials Center .... (800) 336-7402
Order on-line at: http://materials.nrahq.org

To join NRA today, or for additional information regarding membership, please call (800) NRA-3888. Your membership dues can be charged to VISA, MasterCard, American Express or Discover.

■■■■ APPENDIX 3: NRA PUBLICATIONS & VIDEOS

The items listed below are some of the various materials available form the National Rifle Association of America (NRA). To inquire about any of these items or to place and order, contact the NRA Program Materials Center by telephoning (800) 336-7402 between 8:30 a.m. – 11:00 p.m. Weekdays, Saturday/ Sunday 10:00 a.m. – 6:00 p.m.

National Rifle Association Gun Safety Rules – An illustrated, multi-color, eight-panel brochure (which unfolds to feature a 16" x 17" gun rules safety poster on the reverse side) explaining the three fundamental rules of gun safety, plus rules for using and storing a gun. Item #14080.

A Parent's Guide to Gun Safety – A brochure explaining parental responsibilities regarding gun safety for children, when and what to teach a child, and basic gun safety rules. Item #12852 PK/25.

Smart & Safe: Handling Your Firearm – Geared for new gun owners, this comprehensive booklet emphasizes responsibility, safe gun handling and an overview of the various types of guns and their actions. Item #11532.

Firearm Safety and the Hunter – An illustrated, 6-panel brochure explaining safe gun handling in the fields and describing field safety rules for hunters. Item #07430.

The Basics of Pistol Shooting – An illustrated, soft-cover handbook explaining pistol parts and terms, types of ammunition, operation of various pistol actions, safety, cleaning, storage, fundamentals of pistol shooting, shooting positions, and improvement of shooting skills. Item #13270.

The Basics of Rifle Shooting – An illustrated, soft-cover handbook explaining rifle parts and terms, types of ammunition, operation of various rifle actions, safety, cleaning, storage, fundamentals of rifle shooting, shooting positions, and improvement of shooting skills. Item #13180.

NRA Junior Rifle Shooting – An illustrated, soft-cover book specifically designed for young shooters. The book not only covers such topics as gun safety, rifle parts, and shooting equipment, but also describes in detail the various rifle shooting positions. Training tips and suggestions for improving skills are also discussed. Item #09450.

The Basics of Shotgun Shooting – An illustrated, soft-cover handbook explaining shotgun parts and terms, types of ammunition, operation of various shotgun actions, safety, cleaning, storage, fundamentals of shotgun shooting, and improvement of shooting skills. Item #13360.

The Skeeters' Guide – A companion for beginning Skeet Shooters. Jam packed with QuickTips to help new shooters learn the game, understand the jargon, and know what to do on all eight shooting stations. 39 pages, Soft-cover. Item #09180.

Fundamentals of Gun Safety (VHS Format Video-tape) – A 10-minute videotape, narrated by Steve Kanaly and Susan Howard of the TV series *Dallas*, explaining the basics of firearm safety with special emphasis on NRA's three fundamental gun safety rules. Suitable for both teenagers and adults. Item #11560.

The Eddie Eagle GunSafe® Program – The Eddie Eagle GunsSafe® Program was developed to teach children what to do if they find a gun in an unsupervised situation, "STOP! Don't Touch. Leave the Area. Tell an Adult." **The Eddie Eagle® Program Brochure** provides and overview of the program and explains program materials. Item #12350. Schools, law enforcement agencies, youth groups and civic organizations may order the materials for a nominal charge. For more information on this program, call The Eddie Eagle GunSafe® Program toll-free number at 1-800-231-0752.

TECHNICAL QUESTIONS:

Receiving answers to technical questions is a privilege reserved for NRA members. (A non-member may submit a question if the inquiry is accompanied by a membership application.) Each question must be in the form of a letter addressed to:

Dope Bag
NRA Publications
11250 Waples Mill Road
Fairfax, VA 22030

Each inquiry must contain the NRA member's code line from his or her membership card or from the mailing label on the *American Rifleman*, *American Hunter* or *America's 1*ST *Freedom* magazine. In addition, each letter must contain a stamped, self-addressed, legal-size envelope.

Inquiries must be limited to one specific question per letter. Questions regarding the value of any type of firearm will not be accepted. Technical or historical questions will **not** be answered by telephone or by FAX machine.

APPENDIX 4: FACTS ABOUT THE NRA

Established in 1871, the National Rifle Association of America (NRA) is a non-profit organization supported entirely by membership fees and by donations from public-spirited citizens.

The NRA does not receive any appropriations from Congress, nor is it a trade organization. It is not affiliated with any firearm or ammunition manufacturers or with any businesses which deal in firearms or ammunition.

Originally formed to promote marksmanship training, the NRA has since reached out to establish a wide variety of activities, ranging from gun safety programs for children and adults to gun collecting and gunsmithing. Hundreds of thousands of law enforcement personnel have received training from NRA Certified Instructors in the firearm skills needed to protect themselves and the public. In addition, clubs enrolled or affiliated with the NRA exist in communities across the nation, teaching youths and adults gun safety, marksmanship, and responsibility while also providing recreational activities.

The membership roster of the NRA has included seven Presidents of the United States, two Chief Justices of the U.S. Supreme Court, and many of America's outstanding diplomats, military leaders, members of Congress, and other public officials.

The NRA cooperates with federal agencies, all branches of the U.S. Armed Forces, and state and local governments that are interested in training and safety programs.

The basic goals of the NRA are to:

- Protect and defend the Constitution of the United States, especially in regard to the Second Amendment right of the individual citizen to keep and bear arms.
- Promote public safety, law and order, and the national defense.
- Train citizens and members of law enforcement agencies and the armed forces in the safe handling and efficient use of firearms.
- Foster and promote the shooting sports at local, state, regional, national, and international levels.
- Promote hunter safety and proper wildlife management.

For additional information about the NRA, including programs, publications, and membership, contact:

> National Rifle Association of America
> 11250 Waples Mill Road
> Fairfax, VA 22030
> Phone: (703) 267-1000
> (Main Switchboard)

APPENDIX 5: NRA SHORT-TERM GUNSMITHING SCHOOLS

NRA-affiliated gunsmithing schools offer a variety of short-term summer courses. Most courses are approximately five days in length, and cover such interesting subjects as: custom 45 accurizing, design and repair of handguns, rifles, and shotguns, firearms restoration, color casehardening, bluing, Parkerizing, etc.

There are currently four NRA-affiliated gunsmithing schools. For information, contact the schools listed below or call NRA Headquarters at (703) 267-1412.

Lassen Community College
Highway 139
P.O. Box 3000
Susanville, CA 96130
(530) 251-8800

Montgomery Community College
1011 Page Street
Troy, NC 27371
(910) 576-6222

Murray State College
1100 South Murray
Tishomingo, OK 73460
(580) 371-2371

Trinidad State Junior College
600 Prospect
Box 319
Trinidad, CO 81082
(719) 846-5631

Special Thanks

This program was made possible, in part, thanks to
a grant from The NRA Foundation and its generous donors.

The NRA Foundation
11250 Waples Mill Road
Fairfax, VA 22030
1-800-423-6894
www.nrafoundation.org
nraf@nrahq.org